gs

This book is dedicated to
Julian Amos Devlin

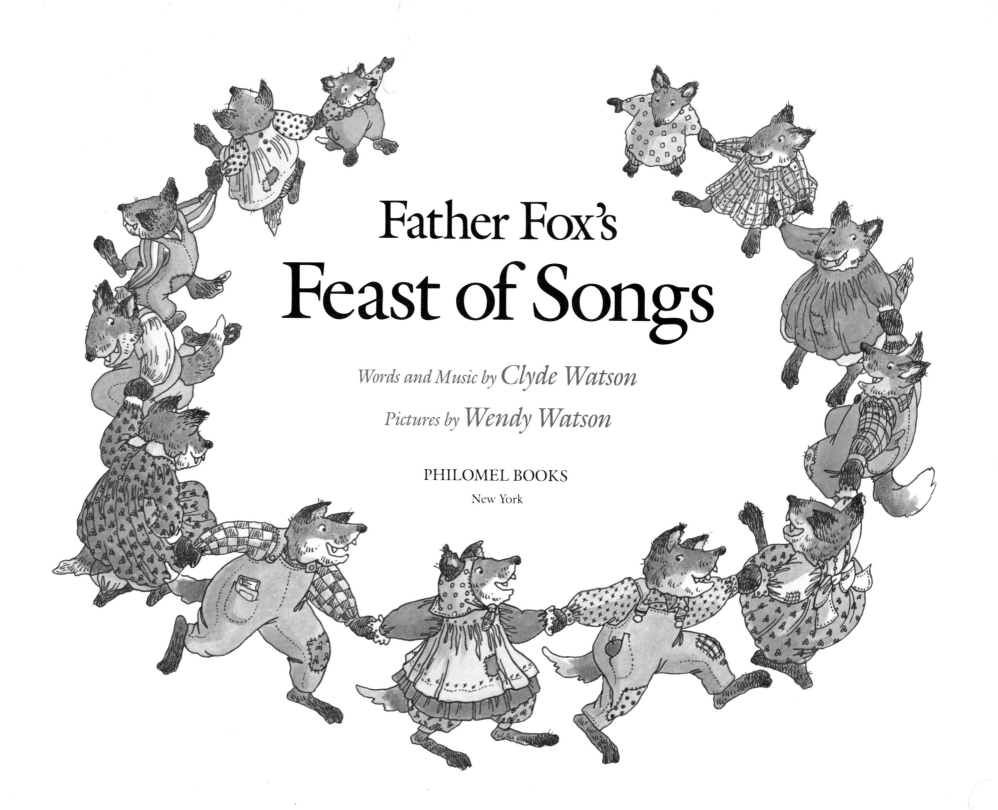

Father Fox's
Feast of Songs

Words and Music by Clyde Watson

Pictures by Wendy Watson

PHILOMEL BOOKS

New York

Words to all of these songs have been published previously in collections of verse.
Here's A Song, Nanny Banny, Oh My Goodness, Huckleberry, Gooseberry,
Uptown, Downtown, Old Tin Cup, Ride Your Red Horse, Soft Falls The Snow,
Belly & Tubs, Mister Lister, Lullabye, and *Bimbo Bombo*
are copyright © 1971 by Clyde Watson, and first appeared in *Father Fox's Pennyrhymes*
published in 1971 by T.Y. Crowell, a division of Harper & Row, New York.
They appear here by permission of T.Y. Crowell. All the others first appeared
in verse form in the collection, *Catch Me & Kiss Me & Say It Again,*
published by Philomel Books (formerly William Collins + World Publishing Company),
a division of The Putnam Publishing Group;
these poems are copyright © 1978 by Clyde Watson.
All rights reserved.

Published by Philomel Books,
a division of The Putnam Publishing Group,
51 Madison Avenue, New York, NY 10010.
Printed in the United States of America.
First edition.

Library of Congress Cataloging in Publication Data
Watson, Clyde.   Father Fox's feast of songs.
For voice and piano; includes chord symbols.
Summary: Twenty-one poems in the style of traditional nursery rhymes, selected from
the author's two earlier collections, with original musical settings for family singing.
1. Children's songs — United States. [1. Songs] I. Watson, Wendy, ill. II. Title.
M1997.W285F4 1983   83-2967
ISBN 0-399-20886-0   ISBN 0-399-20928-X (pbk.)

Contents

2313089

Here's A Song

Sweetly

Here's a song of Tin-ker and Pe - ter, Hon-ey is sweet but love is sweet-er—

What comes next now tell me dear - ly, Al - ex - an - der dar - ling.

Butterprint

Flowing

But-ter-print knocks at the milk-shop door__ What will he have to-day,__ A rose-bud, a dump-ling, a nip-per-kin of milk, then But-ter-print's on his way.

Pig Song

C7   F   Fdim7   B♭   F   Dm7

This lit - tle pig said "Nice sweet let-tuce," This lit-tle pig said_ "Here comes the farm-er!" This lit-tle pig said_

C7   F   Dm   B♭   Gm   F   C7   F

"Bet-ter run or he'll get us!"   But_ this lit - tle pig said "Wee, wee, wee, you can't catch me!"

Oh My Goodness

Punchy

C   G7   Cdim 7

Oh my good-ness, oh my dear,_ Sas - sa - fras and gin-ger beer,_ Choc'-late cake and

F   D7   G7   C   F   C

ap - ple punch:_ I'm too full to eat my lunch, too full to eat my_ lunch.

Huckleberry, Gooseberry

Moderately

Huck-le-ber-ry, goose-ber-ry, rasp-ber-ry pie. All sweet-est things one can-not buy.

Moderately

Pep-per-mint can-dies are six for a pen-ny, But true love and kiss-es, one can-not buy an-y.

Dilly Dilly

With pep

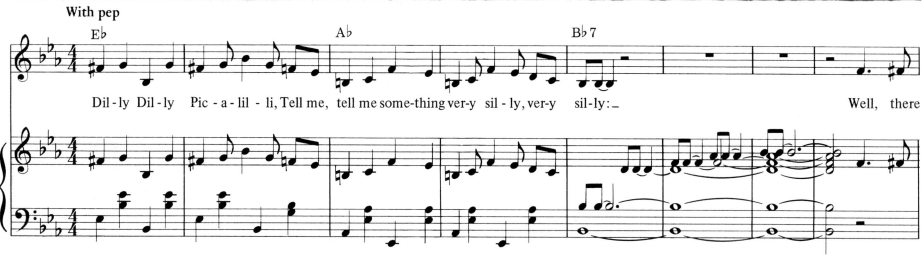

Dil - ly Dil - ly Pic - a - lil - li, Tell me, tell me some-thing ver-y sil - ly, ver-y sil-ly:_ Well, there

Eb dim 7   Ab   Eb   Bb 7   Eb

was a chap, his name was Bert,— He ate the but-tons, ate the but-tons, ate the but-tons off his shirt, off his shirt!

Piggy Back Song

Rolling

Off we go on a pig-gy back ride Far and fan-cy free ___ A-

round the world on an emp-ty purse_ And back in time for tea. ___

Old Tin Cup

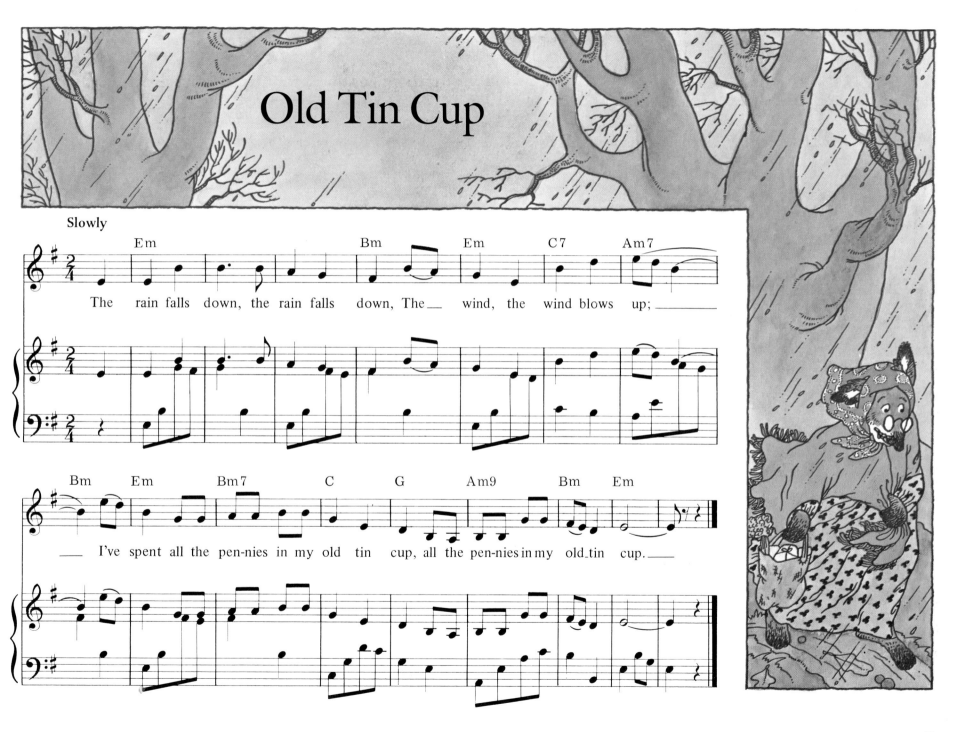

Slowly

The rain falls down, the rain falls down, The___ wind, the wind blows up;___

___ I've spent all the pen-nies in my old tin cup, all the pen-nies in my old_tin cup.___

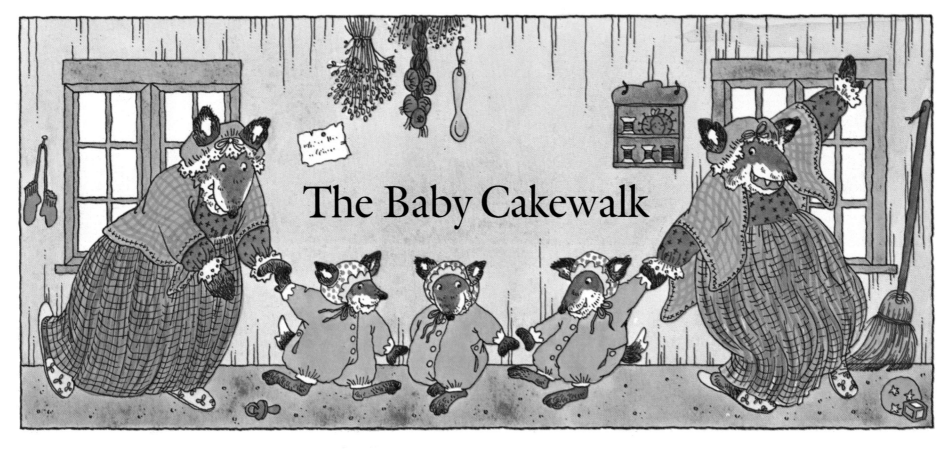

The Baby Cakewalk

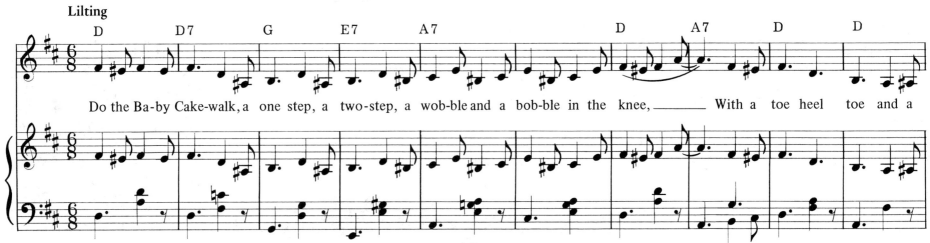

Lilting

Do the Ba-by Cake-walk, a one step, a two-step, a wob-ble and a bob-ble in the knee, _____ With a toe heel toe and a

gid-dy-go-round you go, Won't you do the Ba-by Cake-walk for me?__ me?_____

Hushabye

Not too slow

1. Hush - a - bye, my dar - ling, Don't you make a peep, __ Lit - tle crea-tures
2. Fish - es in the mill - pond, Gos-lings in the barn, __ Kit - ten by the
3. Lis - ten to the rain-drops sing-ing you to sleep, __ Hush - a - bye, my

ev - 'ry-where are set - tling down to sleep.
fire - side, __ Ba - by in my arms.
dar - ling, __ Don't you make a peep.

Belly & Tubs

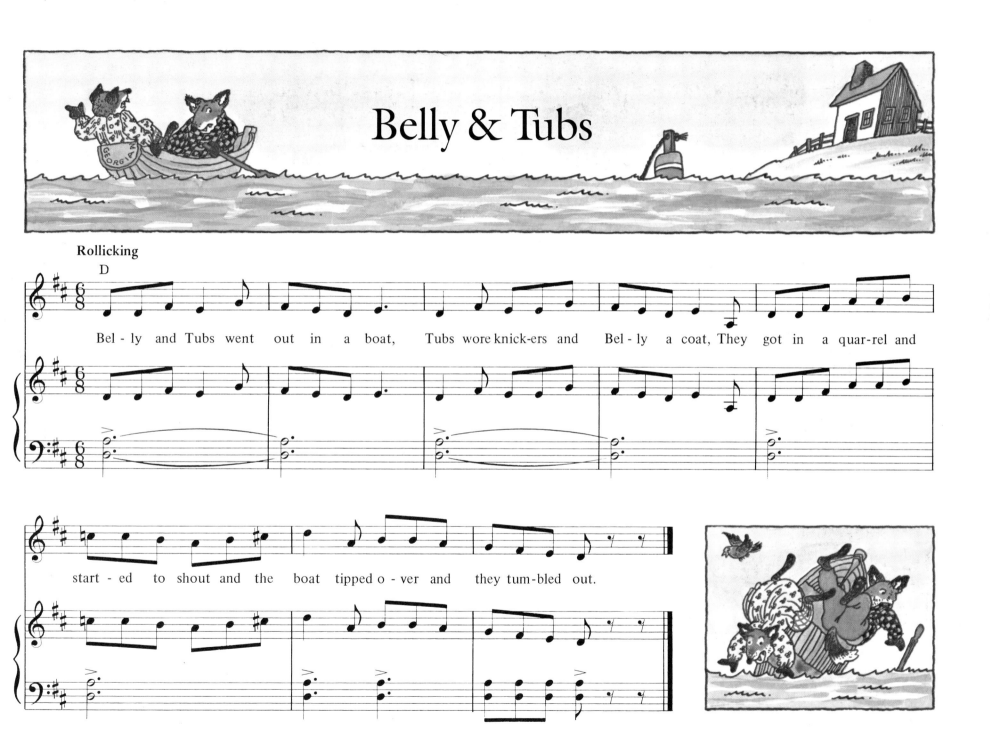

Rollicking

Bel - ly and Tubs went out in a boat, Tubs wore knick-ers and Bel - ly a coat, They got in a quar-rel and start - ed to shout and the boat tipped o - ver and they tum-bled out.

Bimbo Bombo

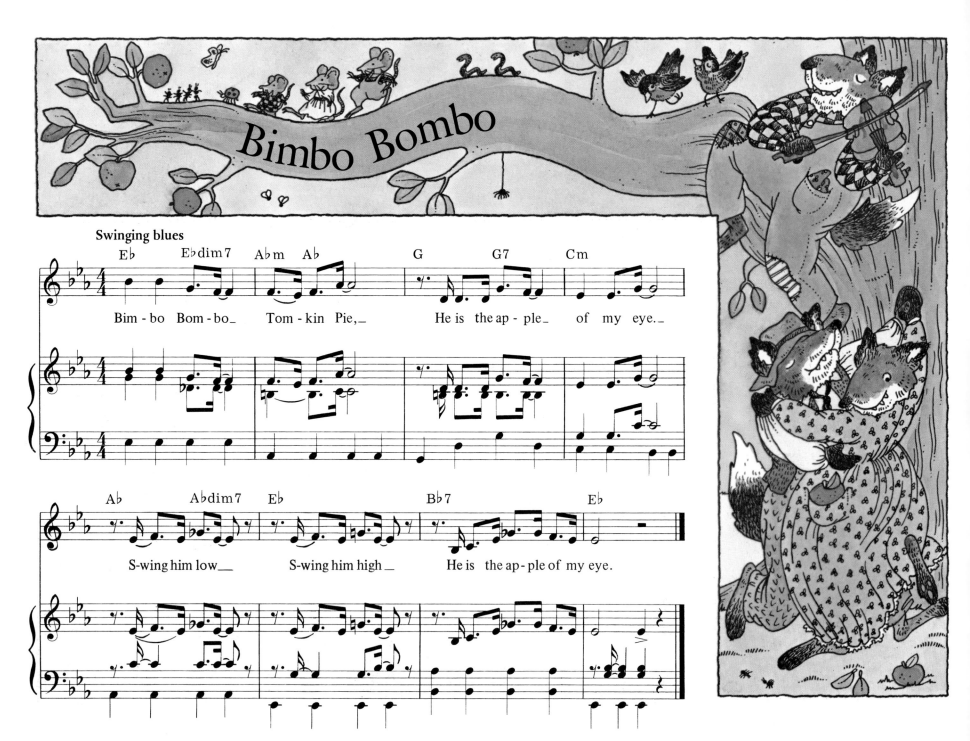

Swinging blues

Eb   Ebdim7   Abm Ab   G   G7   Cm

Bim - bo Bom - bo_ Tom - kin Pie,_ He is the ap - ple_ of my eye._

Ab   Abdim7   Eb   Bb7   Eb

S-wing him low__ S-wing him high _ He is the ap - ple of my eye.

Nanny Banny

Waltzing

Nan-ny Ban-ny Bum-ble bee, Nan-ny is my cup of _ tea. _____

I'm as hap-py as can be When _ I've got Nan-ny on my knee.

Ride Your Red Horse

Lullabye

Softly

Rock, rock, sleep, my ba - by, sleep the whole night through.
Hush, hush, sleep, my ba - by, sings the sweet cuck - oo.

When your dad - dy comes back home he'll bring a toy for you. _____
When your dad - dy comes back home he'll sing a song for you. _____

Mister Lister

Mis – ter Lis – ter sassed his sis – ter, Mar-ried his wife be – cause he couldn't re-sist her

Three plus four times two he kissed her: How man – y times is that, dear sis – ter? that?

See Saw

Miss Quiss

Saucy and quick

Miss Quiss! Look at this! A pock-et full of lic-or-ice! You may have some

If you wish, But ev-'ry stick will cost a kiss! kiss!

Down Derry Down

Lilting

Down der-ry down, my Pip-pin, my Clown, Up-set the ap-ple cart go-ing to town, But we'll

pick up the ap-ples and dust off your hat and sing, All fine and dan-dy-o! just like that.

Uptown, Downtown

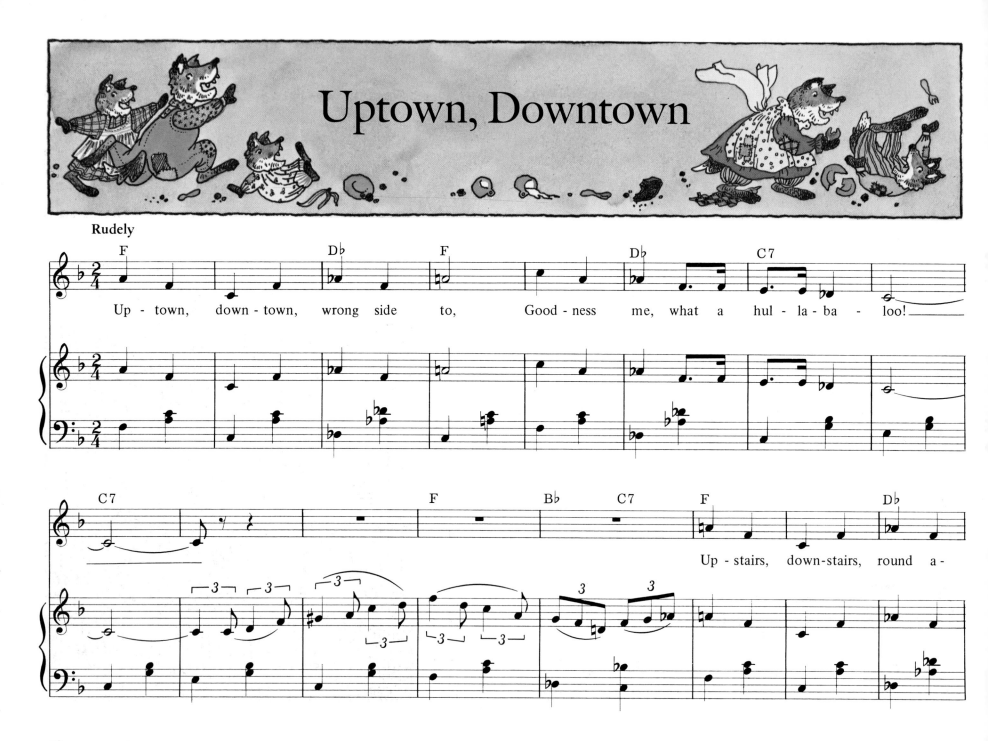

Rudely

Up - town, down - town, wrong side to, Good - ness me, what a hul - la - ba - loo!

Up - stairs, down-stairs, round a-

F · Db · C7 · F

bout, Back - wards, for - wards, in - side __ out!

F · Bbm7 · C7 · F

Soft Falls The Snow

Slowly

Soft falls the snow, the coals burn low, Lit-tle Ja-cob's a - sleep on my knee; _____ My

sto-ry ends here _____ For mid-night is near: To bed now, one, two, ___ three! _____

Clyde and Wendy Watson are sisters, two of eight multitalented children of a well-known poet and a distinguished illustrator and book designer. Their first collaboration, FATHER FOX'S PENNYRHYMES, was hailed as a modern American classic, and its companion book CATCH ME & KISS ME & SAY IT AGAIN was equally popular. *Clyde Watson,* who wrote the poems and the music in FATHER FOX'S FEAST OF SONGS, majored in music at Smith College. She plays the violin professionally in addition to composing. A former teacher, she is the mother of two young children, a son and a daughter, and lives in New Hampshire.

Wendy Watson, a graduate of Bryn Mawr College, has illustrated more than fifty books, some of which she has written herself. Her pictures for this book are done in a combination of pen and ink with watercolor. With her two children, Ms. Watson lives in Vermont.